"I Love You,"
signed Jesus

Surprising studies into the sufferings of
Jesus — God's love at its most intimate
and expressive moment.

Ray W. Lincoln

Copyright 2006, by Ray W. Lincoln
Copyright 2007, first revised edition, printed in the United States of America
Copyright 2009, first revised edition, second printing, printed in the United States of America
Copyright 2017, first revised edition, third printing, printed in the United States of America

ISBN: 978-0-9961208-7-6 (Paperback)

Published in the United States of America
Apex Publications
Littleton, CO
October of 2017

Dedication

To the one who has enriched my earthly existence with her love;
Filled my closest relationship with its warmth;
Walked with me through dark valleys and sacrificed;
Comforted me with love's fire.
To my dearest treasure, my wife, Mary Jo.

Also, to a man whose example and academic excellence challenged me and changed my path, and led me to a study of this holy subject.

To the memory of Professor E. M. Blaiklock

Acknowledgements

I am grateful to Professor E. M. Blaiklock for the inspiration and initial impetus for my study in this area. It was a comment of his that led me to the work of Drs. Barbet, La Bec, and Hynek.

I am also grateful for happening upon a rare work of Karl Bornhaeuser, dealing with the textual and background material for the passion of Christ, which was translated into English by A. Rumpus of Kotagiri, South India. The insights gained have provided me with much of the detail and confirmation for the interpretations in this book. He was a dedicated exegete and a brilliant linguist.

I am grateful to my wife, Mary Jo, for her labors with the manuscript.

CONTENTS

"I LOVE YOU," signed Jesus

The sufferings of Jesus examined medically and textually

Introduction

The rallying cry of missionary enterprise, "The love of Christ constrains us," has rung through the centuries and emboldened many to sacrifice and suffer. The cross of Christ, more than the empty tomb, has become Christianity's central motif. And the reason is, perhaps, the vivid display of love the cross offers to a puzzled world. We may not understand the theology of the cross; but we respond to its display of love.

We long for love. Our frames seem built to hang its flesh. And flesh is what it feels like — warm and comforting, fondling and engaging our passions for acceptance. Love calls us, woos us and wins us from all other enticements. Love is what we want most. So, when we discover a God — **the** God — who actually loves us, we can't believe it. We also can't believe it when we fail to feel that love. God's love, which should be the greatest feeling we ever welcomed, seems to most people so far away and unreal. It feels otherworldly, as though it belongs to some unnamed universe far, far from our pained passions.

But Jesus, a human — one of us and divine to boot — brings it right home into our hearts. He loves in our flesh. He breathes our air and suffers with our pain; and to see him endure suffering for us is to be enlightened at the same time that we are blessed with the realizable human expression of this the highest of all loves.

> ✝
> *He loves in our flesh. He breathes our air and suffers with our pain …*

It's the love of Jesus that drives him to die for us, that makes the God of the Bible so very, very attractive. To appreciate that love even more and from a new perspective we will journey together through his sufferings — from the

Garden of Gethsemane to a few moments after his last breath on the cross. We will feel our way into his heart; shout with anger at his enemies; weep at the truth that, but for the grace of God, there go I; and, like the people of his day, reject the one who loves us most.

Scientific and Textual Help

✝

Our increased knowledge of the suffering of Christ is due to archaeological, medical and linguistic studies.

In the last 66 years, our understanding of the extent of Christ's love for us has increased greatly. It's this new understanding that I want to pass on to you. My prayer is that it will light a warm fire in your heart and mind, too.

Our increased knowledge of the suffering of Christ is due to archaeological, medical and linguistic studies. Such names as Barbet, Hynek, La Bec, Holzmeister, Blaiklock and Bornhaeuser — four of whom are devoted Roman Catholics and whose love for Jesus is patently obvious — are instrumental in bringing to us many of these surprising findings. I have added just a few textual details, which have not found much light of day, from the study of the Greek texts.

I have used lay terms instead of the more accurate medical terms where I felt it would benefit the reader and where I had no brief lay description, I stayed with the medical term.

In the Olive Groves

We will begin in the dark shadows of the gnarled olive trees in the Garden of Gethsemane. Gethsemane (the word means the "garden of the oil press") stood on the opposing slope of the Kidron Valley from where the upper room was located in a Jerusalem street. It is dark, but not too dark to see. And the air around seems heavy with its own intuition of what is about to take place.

The time? - A little after midnight on Thursday, the night before Jesus died. The disciples who are with him and who have dined with him till near the middle of the night (as was the custom for this preparation meal for the Passover) are tired and sleepy. They rest under the olive branches. Their rest is shallow. The heavy meal lingered in their stomachs and the emotions raised by Jesus' puzzling words un-eased them, too. Something about their Master's look, actions, and emotions, was otherworldly — almost alien — and they couldn't put their fingers on it. Was this the end of which he so embarrassingly had spoken? He asked Peter, James and John to watch with him as he prayed. Even to them the atmosphere was tense with a foreboding that created their anxiety.

There was nothing alarming in the midnight stroll to this familiar place. *"Jesus went out as usual to the Mount of Olives, and his disciples followed him,"* Luke casually writes. The irregular occurred when they got there. He asked the three to pray while he prayed, and then he walked a stone's throw further into the dim shadows of the trees. The separation seemed appropriate. He was feeling all the more alone over the past days as he prepared his heart and mind for this moment. The gap between him and his

> ✝
> *The gap between him and his disciples was wider than the stone's throw suggested. Minds and hearts were in different worlds.*

3

disciples was wider than the stone's throw suggested. Minds and hearts were in different worlds. Kneeling down, he prayed a startling prayer, "Father, if you are willing, take this cup from me; yet not my will, but yours be done."

The Beginnings of Suffering

"An angel appeared to him and strengthened him," Luke tells us. This occurrence marks the beginnings of the unusual events that were about to take place before the disciple's eyes. At this point they must have been watching, as it was obvious that Jesus was deep in anguish, and the following report could have come from no others. All the details are not told; but as is common to the writers of the Gospels, only the bare facts are revealed to us and we are left in curious frustration for further answers. However, the details we were meant to know are hidden in the text. We must find them.

Luke 22:44 states, "And being in anguish, he prayed more earnestly..." The degree of concern is hinted at in the word anguish (ayonia), a word that occurs only here in the New Testament. You can guess its meaning because our word "agony" comes from it. The word could be translated as effort, excitement, alarm or anxiety, which were its early meanings in Greek literature (as early as Aristotle). Or it could mean fear, as expressed by Philo and Josephus who lived centuries later. In that case, we would translate, "And being afraid..." If, however, we cross reference it with Hebrews 5:7, "During the days of Jesus' life on earth, he offered up prayers and petitions with loud cries and tears to the one who would save him from death,

> ✝
> He was fighting a battle inside of himself that was wrenching at his heart and causing its precious love to be spilled in a way we have not seen in his life thus far.

4

and he was heard because of his reverent submission," we might translate it with the words "As he fought with death." It is clear this was no ordinary struggle. He was fighting a battle inside of himself that was wrenching at his heart and causing its precious love to be spilled in a way we have not seen in his life thus far.

Suddenly, Luke writes the next phrase and we are stopped in our tracks with a myriad of questions: *"...and his sweat was like drops of blood falling to the ground."* (Some early manuscripts omit verses **43** and **44**, but there is insufficient textual warrant to omit them. Only the apparent absurdity of their claim makes them suspect to some scholars; but we will explain their mystery).

Who ever heard of sweat like drops of blood? Worse still, the Greek word for "drops" is not a word meaning drops at all. The

> ✝
> *"...and his sweat was like drops of blood falling to the ground."*

word Luke uses is the Greek word *thromboi*, from which we get our English words thrombosis, thrombotic and thrombus. They all mean a "clot" of blood — not a "drop" of blood. Thrombosis is the clotting of blood. In fact, the Greek word here means a clot of curdled blood. Father Lagrange translates it accurately with the word "globules."

No wonder it has been translated "drop" in most of the versions; because whoever heard of clots of blood being sweat and falling to the ground? The seeming absurdity deepens. The translators must have felt compelled to translate "drop" since "clot" would be beyond all credibility.

Luke, you will remember, was a medical doctor, trained in observation, interview and analysis. To him it was important to record the facts as observed, and he did so, although he, too, must have been mystified at his own words.

III with Hematidrosis

Until very recently, we had no answer for this strange phenomenon. But we can now identify this medical condition as hematidrosis. Hematidrosis is extremely rare. I mean very, very rare. The capillaries just under the surface of the skin become extremely distended and, in contact with the sweat glands, they burst. The blood mingles with the sweat and oozes to the surface of the skin where, in contact with the air, it coagulates. You now have clots of blood on the skin's surface. This condition, however, occurs over the whole surface of the skin and would have been visible to the disciples after his prayer had finished. As the sweating persists the clots of mingled blood and sweat fall to the ground. Luke's faithful questioning of the disciples (his source for the information), and his insistence at recording the observation as reported, has been justified. And today we are able to understand more about the extent of our Lord's suffering in that garden before the painful torment of the cross ever began.

We also know what causes hematidrosis, and what the effects of it are on the human system. We are not talking "upset." This is a place where I can safely say, since it is so rare, none of us have probably ever been. It is caused by extreme mental and emotional torment. Truly an internal fight with death; we are here reaching the outer limits of a human's capacity to suffer. It is nothing short of an internal eruption; a bursting of the dam of emotions, ending in a torrent of pain that wounds severely as it rushes through the mind and body.

> ✝
> "My soul is exceeding sorrowful even unto death."

He even said, *"My soul is exceeding sorrowful, even unto death!"* He felt like the pain in his soul would kill him. Mark, reporting Peter's memory, says, *"He began to fear and to be heavy."* *"Sorely amazed or afraid"* is perhaps a better rendering, but afraid of what? We find a clue as he cries in agony, *"Take this cup from me..."* We shall never know the full extent or nature of the agony *this cup* contained; but

> ✝
> *...we are here reaching the outer limits of a human's capacity to suffer.*

we know it was enough to crush and break all lesser spirits. It spilled physical, emotional, and spiritual pain unbearable. We can deduce from other New Testament comments that Jesus was faced with becoming sin for us; faced with being what he was not — with becoming the very thing his nature could not bear. **The cross might as well have already happened, so intense was this pre-Calvary anguish.**

What of the after effects of hematidrosis? First, it causes a serious loss of blood; secondly, a severe fall in vital resistance; and, thirdly, the skin becomes very sensitive, tender and painful to the touch.

Are we beginning to understand that this voluntary journey he was taking to the cross was propelled by some great power inside him? Some strong desire that would not let him quit?

In This Condition He Suffered Arrest and Violent Attacks

In this physical and mental state — a very sick man — he was roughly arrested and bundled off to trial in the wee hours of the morning. To be touched — let alone grabbed and mauled — was galling. The trial itself was illegal, happening as it did during the night hours and lasting into the early hours of daylight. Let alone the clear directions in Jewish law in regard to witnesses, the trial seemed out of control. The witnesses were, according to Jewish law, to be admonished by the court and then removed and brought in, one-at-a-time, to hear their

7

accusations. If the various witnesses did not agree (which was the case in Jesus' trial), the judge was to throw out their evidence or testimony. He did not! The trial was a farce. Read it for yourself.

John 18:23 reports violence. In fact, **all four accounts record the presence of violence in the trial.** Physical persuasion was being used to extract a confession — surely illegal. They struck him with their fists. How that must have hurt! Matthew 26:67 says they slapped him with the palms of their hands — not as violent, if we accept

> ✝
> *Considerable damage would have been inflicted on skin so tender and bleeding.*

this translation; but, for Jesus, excruciating none-the-less. It was Jerome who started translating this Greek word, *rapisma*, as slaps rather than blows. Its real meaning is better translated here in Matthew 26:67 as "struck with their hands," suggesting a blow rather than a mere slap.

John 19:3 agrees with Matthew 27:30, using the same word (*rapisma*), which in its common usage meant to be struck with a stick. It even sounds like the rap of a blow with a stick – *rapisma!* And all this in a condition of extreme sensitivity to touch. Considerable damage would have been inflicted on skin so tender and bleeding. I can't get away from the question "Why does he put up with their humiliating hate? Does he love me that much?"

> ✝
> *This was the God/man offering his love and forgiveness to his human creatures even while they ravaged him with a bitterness born of fermenting fury.*

We will never know the pain he went through, while at the same time exemplifying remarkable poise bolstered by a divine love. This was the God/man offering his love and forgiveness to his human creatures even while they ravaged him with a bitterness born of fermenting fury.

The continuous beating, torture and embarrassment of the trial were calculated to subdue the victim and gain a conviction from their lips or a reaction that was culpable. Try as they may, they only documented their venomous envy and their desperate irrational methods to convict him.

With his condition further weakened by the beatings and rough treatment, they turned to perhaps the most despicable, depraved, disgusting, mortifying thing a person can do: they spat in his face! Spitting in the face of God! Yes! Neurotic thinkers and evil hearts will attempt the humiliation of God with hell-bent velocity and without apparent fear. A God of irrepressible anger would have come unglued and consigned them to a thousand hells. But we are watching a God of remarkable forbearance and love. We are learning the lesson of divine care — of forgiveness, "for they don't know what they are doing."

The Scourging

After about six hours of venomous hatred, strangely tempered by confusion as to how they could incriminate him, the illegal trial ended in binding him and leading him to Pilate. It was about seven or eight o'clock in the morning now. Pilate had risen and eaten, and they knew that only then would he entertain their intrusions. Hence, their reluctant delay.

Another farce of a trial before Pilate evolved before our eyes. Pilate was desperate. He was influenced by his wife's dream and her recommendation that he have nothing to do with this righteous man. To complicate Pilate's decision, it seems that in an unrecorded earlier meeting, he had apparently given the Jewish leaders the understanding that he would forgo a formal trial and simply serve a warrant for death. Their confusion was reflected in their answer to the regular words opening a formal trial, "What accusation do you bring against this man?" and it gives them away. They replied with an unprepared stutter: "If this man was not an evil-doer we would not have brought him to you," — hardly a clear charge! They were not expecting a formal trial and he caught them without a formally prepared charge. Pilate seemed to be reneging on an agreement.

He was trapped now, just as they were, and delayed all he could. The Jewish leaders, however, needed a hasty execution because of the approaching Passover, and Pilate knew it. In typical fashion, he was spiting them, but it wasn't going to work to his favor.

Pilate took Jesus and flogged him in the hope that this would pacify the crowd and that they would accept it as a substitute for the death verdict. It could have worked. A scourging was the next worst fate to death by crucifixion.

Flogging was legally inflicted to within one lash before the victim died. It was calculated variously — often 39 stripes. The victim was then left to live or die. Only the demonic torture of the cross caused more pain. If he died from the scourging, they would maintain, it was the judgment of God and not their miscalculations.

> ✝
> *Only the demonic torture of the cross caused more pain.*

But watch with me a moment before you turn away sick in heart and stomach. The soldier is holding a wooden handle, about 2 feet (60 cm) long, to which is attached from 2 to 7 leather thongs that are up to 6 feet (180 cm) in length. At approximately 6 inch (15 cm) intervals the thongs are knotted. Inserted in the knots are small rocks, or sticks, or pieces of bone (often the talus bones of a sheep). The purpose of the inserts was to lacerate the flesh, and the knots are to bruise and pulverize the victim.

The soldier drew back and, with calloused glee, powerfully using the centrifugal force of the movement, lashed the victim with all his might. As the scourge wrapped itself around the body, he drew it back tearing at the flesh. Blow after blow thumped the body mercilessly. Each stripe increasingly caused distress, and slowly, numbness from partial loss of consciousness (the numbness is a medical opinion), came to Jesus' relief — but not for long. The pain returned with a vengeance. In this way, his back and legs were insufferably laid open with cannibalistic glee. *"Hail King of the Jews,"* they cried. Chrysostom, a bishop around 400 AD, in his disgust of their violence, called the soldiers "nothing but bloodthirsty dogs." In contrast we hear the cry of Jesus from the cross, *"Father, forgive them, for they know not what they do."* If this is love, it is alien to selfish hearts and known only to those who recognize God's heart.

> ✝
> *...his back and legs were insufferably laid open with cannibalistic glee.*

The Crown of Thorns

As if this were not "fun" enough, they plaited a crown of thorns and pushed it down on his head. Here, our understanding has been led astray by the artists who show the crown of thorns as a wreath of thorns, wrapped in a band around the head. Rather, it was a "cap" of thorns, plaited to puncture the entire surface of the head that a cap would cover.

Could he bear any more? Is there any wonder that, already ill and stressed to the limits of human suffering, he is unable to carry the patibulum (the horizontal arm of the cross)? And as we will soon see, the worst by far was yet to come.

Pilate played his last desperate card before he lost the game to an enraged, bloodthirsty crowd. *"Who do you want me to release to you? Jesus or Barabbas?"* he asks. (Barabbas was an insurrectionist — we would say a terrorist — killing without distinction both Roman and Jew). He gave the **people,** not the Jewish leaders, the choice. But in a land where, now as then, fierce nationalism and racial hatred burn like a fire and terrorists become heroes overnight, Barabbas was chosen to live. We are not surprised.

Via Dolorosa

Leading him out, they placed the patibulum across his shoulders. The stipes, the vertical pole of the cross, was already at the place of crucifixion, standing in its socket in the ground. Each arm of the victim was extended and strapped to the patibulum. **It was part of the victim's disgrace that he was forced to carry his own cross** (patibulum) to the place where he would die.

This cross piece was no small piece of lumber. It weighed about seventy to one hundred pounds (35 to 55 kilograms), and was roughly hewn from a log. Its course surface would further have aggravated the wounds caused by the flogging. Staggering along, Jesus' severely mangled (though muscular) frame was quite unable to carry it. He fell. How far he got we do not know. Simon of Cyrene, who had come from afar to celebrate the Passover (the aim of every Jew of the dispersion to accomplish at least once in his lifetime), happened to be too near and was forced to carry it while Jesus was "helped" to the place of the skull. The "help" would not have been compassionate.

For Simon, this was a disaster! His much anticipated journey was for naught now. He was ceremonially defiled because he carried a condemned man's cross and would not be able to participate in the Passover, which was the whole purpose of his pilgrimage. His life-long dream was spoiled. I wonder what he did and thought. Was he angry? Or did his life change forever because of his contact with Jesus? Just maybe Mark's identification of Simon of Cyrene's offspring in Mark 15:21 (a note that otherwise would mean little) and also because probably the same people are mentioned in the letter to the Romans (since the names are the same) might indicate that he became a follower of Jesus. It is conjecture, admittedly. But at least it is interestingly possible.

In the little town of San Luis, high in a large mountain valley in Colorado, a trail leaves the main street and winds its way up a hill to the town's Catholic chapel on the top. Along the way are magnificent bronze statues of the events of the Via Dolorosa, one of them being Jesus' falling under the weight of the patibulum. The sculpture is beautifully and realistically expressive of the agony of Jesus and of his lacerated body. To see it is to worship the God who offers such love to the callous torturers of his heart.

Mt. Calvary

The location of the crucifixion is a matter for scholars. It is most likely Gordon's Calvary; but, whether or not, it was "the place of the skull" — Golgotha. Many crucifixions had taken place there. History would suggest hundreds, if not more. The skulls of some were left to bleach on the rocky outcrop, and hence the name.

Nails Through His Wrists

Arriving at Golgotha with a crowd in tow (which no doubt included Mary [his mother], John, Matthew and Peter), they threw Jesus on the ground. (The accounts of the disciples, who provided first-hand reports of what happened, are in their respective Gospels). Stretching out his arms, they prepared to nail his hands to the patibulum that lay on the ground. Had he carried the patibulum, they would have nailed his hands to the timber and then removed the ropes that lashed it to his outstretched arms. With no resistance and an obviously weakened victim, their task was easy. The nails were rugged, four-sided pieces of metal, hammered in with large mallets. With the victim in a supine position the nail could be accurately placed and aimed. They would need to do that. These executioners were experts at securing a body firmly to the cross.

If the nails were driven through the palm of the hand (where most artists show us that he was nailed), the weight of a human body would tear the flesh out between the fingers and the victim would be free. Professional soldiers would not make such an amateurish mistake. In fact, to be certain that this would be the result of being nailed through the palm of the hand, tests were conducted in France on amputated limbs while applying 100 pounds of weight — much less than a male body. The nail pulled out through the fingers. I squirm a little at the thought. However, we feel we can know for certain that Jesus was not nailed to the cross through the palms of the hands — as painful as that might be. A more cruel torture had, of necessity, been designed.

If you bend your wrist backwards and run your finger along the bend at the end of the forearm and the beginning of the hand, you will find a small hollow. This is where the professional soldier, who had done this a thousand times, would skillfully exit the nail from the hand. Holding your finger on that spot and straightening out your wrist, you can ascertain where, on the opposite side of the wrist, the point of the nail would be placed to exit at that predetermined point. You can also find a hollow on the main crease that marks the bend of the wrist on the inside of the hand. This is the entry point.

Why at this place in the wrist? Because, if a nail is placed at this hollow and given a strong blow with a large hammer (such as would be done by an executioner), the nail finds a passageway as it forces the bones apart and slides, without fail and without crushing any of the bones of the hand, to exit at the point I have described. The place is generally known as Destot's space. It is the only place in the hand that will securely hold the person to the cross.

Now, this is perhaps worth a comment, since the psalmist said, *"Not a bone of him shall be broken"* [Psalm 34:20]. John draws our attention to this prediction when he notes that Jesus' legs were not broken [John 19:36]. To some, this may not mean anything. To others, it will be a remarkable fact, adding yet another seemingly impossible accurate detail to prophecies spoken centuries before.

The Moment of Deepest Physical Agony.

The nail, in passing through Destot's space, would sever or damage the median nerves. They are not only the motor nerves that operate the thumb and fingers, but they are also the main sensory nerves. When the arm is extended these nerves are strung tight, and damage to them would result in one of the worst tortures that is imaginable to a human. Without some sort of temporary respite (such as a fainting fit), it would be so intense that it is not likely that life would be sustained. **Barbet (a surgeon) indicates, also, that this is one of the most terrible forms of human suffering.** Even under an anesthetic, it causes a serious fall in arterial tension.

> ✝
> The nail, in passing through Destot's space, would sever or damage the median nerves.

15

Knowingly, just before they nailed their victims to the patibulum, the soldiers would offer them a mixture of wine and gall to help lessen the pain they were about to endure. The first three Gospels record the offer and tell how Jesus, having tasted it, refused to drink it. Why? Not because it contained wine and he was not going to drink alcohol. He had drunk wine before. In fact, he had made it for a wedding celebration. The reason seems most likely to be that he did not want to be drugged. It was his plan that, if the Father did not take this cup (the cup of suffering) from him, he would drink it — all of it. And drink the fullness of agony he did. Love is given a new, unearthly meaning in Jesus.

I can't imagine how, after all he had already suffered, he could have born this. I can only register my most meaningful and intense worship as I gaze on a cross and remember that this was for me. How can it possibly be that I am so important to Jesus as to keep him bent on saving me via a path through the kind pain of which I know nothing and wish never to encounter?

> ✝
> *It was his plan that, if the Father did not take this cup (the cup of suffering) from him, he would drink it — all of it. And drink the fullness of agony he did.*

Textually, a small matter needs clarification. John 20:27 invites Thomas to reach out his finger and place it in the mark in his hands. Psalm 22:16 says, *"They have pierced my hands..."* Some have insisted that this means the palm of the hand and not the wrist. I can think of no good reason why the wrist cannot be regarded also as the hand. The precise spot I have mentioned is anatomically regarded as the hand. I think this is calling for a literalism that condemns itself by its insistence on its own limited understanding of a word that can and does have a wider usage.

Stigmatists

Perhaps of greater importance is the stigmata of those that have claimed to have had repeated appearances of the wounds of Christ in their hands, such as St. Francis of Assisi. In their cases they bleed in the palms of the hands, not the wrists. In deference to those to whom this is an important matter, I refer them to the words of Theresa Neumann, who says that we are not to think that the Savior had his wounds where she has hers: in the palms of her hands. Her marks, she claims, have only mystical meaning, adding that Jesus must have been more firmly fixed to the cross.

Dropping the Patibulum in Its Place

It would hurt anyone who can empathize with the suffering of others to think of the next brutal movement. Supine on the ground and suffering the worst pain he would have to endure, two soldiers grabbed the ends of the patibulum and dragged his body with it as they raise it and then dropped it into the socket in the top of the stipes!

Feeling the weight of his body on the nails, once again aggravating the median nerve as they lifted him up, would be excruciating beyond understanding. Then, to be dropped into the socket was callous cruelty at its worst. Recite these words as you read to understand why.

Amidst a rabble's cry,
A man went forth to die
For you, for me.

Bloodstained his every tread;
Cross-laden, on he sped
For you, for me.

I know why he did it. He did it for me. Magnificent love!

The Shape of The Cross

It almost seems sacrilegious to destroy our centuries-old concept that the cross of Jesus formed the shape of our lower case "t". The artists first foisted the idea on us. Then everyone followed. Now we hang a cross in the shape of the lower case "t" around our necks, wear it to adorn clergy robes, embroider it on our clothing or use it to identify our churches, and think it correctly symbolizes the cross of Christ. Not so.

The cross was the shape of the <u>upper</u> case letter "T." The patibulum fitted into a mortise and tenon joint of sorts on the top of the upright piece, the stipes. As we have already noted, the stipes was left to stand at the place of crucifixion, fitted into a hole in the ground. What perhaps caused the artists to represent the cross as a lower case "t" was the practice of attaching to the stipes a notice that would project above the head and be read by the passer by. We know this is what was done to the cross of Jesus. But remember, the cross was the shape of the upper case "T".

The Nailing of the Feet

Having dropped the patibulum in its socket, they then nailed the feet to the cross. This was done by bending the knees so that the soles of the feet were flat against the stipes. What we must envisage at this point is the sinking of the body so as to cause the arms to be extended at an upward angle due to the weight of the body. Then crossing one foot over the other, one nail was driven through the two feet to secure them to the cross. No particular place can be determined for the nail. The crucified could then push himself upward, enduring the pain in the feet as they pressed against the nail, to relieve the pressure on the hands. A horrible compromise!

18

To some crosses (but not to the cross on which they crucified Jesus), a sedile (basically, a block of wood) would be nailed to serve as a seat for the victim. It was used to prolong the time the victim would likely hang on the cross. As it was only hours until the beginning of the sacred observance of Passover, this would have been a most unlikely addition.

Traumatic Pericarditis

The evidence of the extent of his sufferings is revealed in another event that happened after he had died. A soldier took a spear and thrust it into his side just to make certain he was indeed dead. Out came blood and water, according to John. This unusual statement is evidence of a direct observation. Theories abound as to what this means. Dr. Stroud suggests that it is the evidence of a broken heart — broken by his great concern for all the people. His medical theory that explains this condition would only apply to a person who already had an unhealthy heart. This theory does not fit Jesus because there is no evidence of cardiac weakness or illness in Jesus.

> ✝
> *The resulting fluids surrounding the heart would have caused horrible pain and added another unbelievable dimension to his sufferings.*

The rush of what looked like blood and water from Jesus' side, to the untrained observer, is best explained as an acute trauma to the heart brought on by scourging, which traumatized the chest area. The resulting fluids surrounding the heart would have caused horrible pain and added another unbelievable dimension to his sufferings. A rupture of this area by a spear after death would have brought about the gush of water and blood that John records, if he had indeed suffered from traumatic pericarditis.

I am at a loss to describe the intensity of our Savior's suffering and the immensity of his love for us in staying the course and drinking to the full the cup the Father had allotted him. Divine love is certainly beyond our capacity to comprehend and fully appreciate. Jesus suffered all this for my salvation? I bow in worship and inexpressible gratitude. It surely brings a full and satisfying meaning to the words, "He died of a broken heart!"

What Was the Actual Cause of Death and Why Did He Die So Quickly?

We turn now to this more academic question, which will reveal the last horrifying phase of the crucifixion.

A Quick Death by Normal Standards

The outlaws on each side of him outlived him and died only because their legs were broken. They had to be removed from their crosses by the beginning of Passover that evening. Most crucified men lasted through the day; some through the night and into the second day. The surprising speed of Jesus' death is perhaps easily explained by the extreme weakness of his condition prior to crucifixion. The ravaging effects of his mental torture on the Mount of Olives, resulting in hematidrosis, would have caused more than a noticeable fall in his resilience and strength. It

> ✝
> …*psychologically, traumas do not* <u>*add*</u> *their pain to each preceding pain. Rather their effect is* <u>*multiplied*</u> *with each additional trauma, causing a progressively faster fall in resistance.*

would have lowered the body's ability to withstand punishment. It alone could account for Jesus' speedy death.

But there was more, much more. The blows from the fists, but particularly the blows with a rod to the head, as Matthew records, may have produced serious concussion (cerebral shock), as the French surgeon, Dr. Barbet, suggests. These and the scourging, followed by the rupture of a large nerve trunk, would cause us to expect a quick death on the cross. And let's not forget that, psychologically, traumas do not add their pain to each preceding pain. Rather their effect is multiplied with each additional trauma, causing a progressively faster fall in resistance. His ability to withstand pain and maintain life would be many, many times less in the last three hours on the cross than immediately after the arrest in the garden, ill though he was from hematidrosis.

However, let's not forget that the moment of his death was self-determined and voluntary. "*He called out, 'It is finished,' and with a loud cry gave up the ghost.*" [John 19:30] So, to the believer, the speedy death is no mystery. It was his plan. However, for the non-believer, the pre-crucifixion sufferings adequately account for it as well.

The One Determining Cause of Death

Lengthy discussions have been conducted and books have been written on the cause of death. Until the studies that led to this book were completed, we were never quite certain as to the scientific cause. We now know for certain what caused the death of crucified victims and it emphasizes the cunning, evil genius of this form of death by torture.

But first, let us dispense with the ideas that have littered the road to this discovery.

Loss of blood

It has been supposed that he died because he lost too much blood. A quick survey of his wounds would seem to suggest this. He lost blood from hematidrosis, the beatings, the scourging, the crown of thorns and the nail wounds. Wouldn't that be enough loss of blood to bring on death? Medically, we are told, no. It would have caused a serious loss of blood and an extreme weakness, but not death. We can confidently say he didn't die from a loss of blood.

Hunger

Some, Eusebius being one, have maintained he died of a lack of food. Not so. People don't die of hunger in the few hours from Thursday evening (when he ate his last meal) to Friday afternoon.

Exposure to the Sun

This was not the peak of summer. It was mid spring and, even in Palestine at this time of year, the heat is not so oppressive as to cause death in less than six hours. It may well have added to the speed of his death, because he would be so dehydrated (from loss of blood and lack of liquid to replenish the loss) as to be effectively weakened.

However, crucified victims died just as certainly on a cloudy day as on a sunny day. We must also remember that, at noon, the sun was darkened for three hours. A storm broke and the heat from the sun vanished until 3PM, giving a welcome relief to soldiers and victims. He died very shortly after this celestial phenomenon had ended. Verdict? It was unlikely to have caused Jesus' death.

Thirst — Taking of Liquid – Then a Seizure, Culminating in Death

Observations of this kind of torture have indicated that profuse sweating takes place. This and the considerable loss of blood would account for his thirst. Remember, he cried, *"I thirst."* The soldiers offered him a sponge soaked in vinegar, which most interpreters of the biblical text think was the ordinary drink that was available to the soldiers and usually always at hand. It was made of water, vinegar and beaten eggs.

Of all the theories that have been offered for the cause of his death, this would perhaps be most likely if it weren't for the fact that we now know, without doubt, what killed crucified victims. Examples are known where people suffering extreme torture have died abruptly from a seizure after taking a little water. Many have not. Medical reasons that we do not need to go into here can be cited for these sudden deaths. This pattern of taking liquid and a sudden death to follow is indeed the way Jesus died. But we can't draw the conclusion that, simply because the pattern existed, that it assures us of the cause of death.

What makes it so unlikely in Jesus' case is that Luke, who was a trained medical doctor, does not even record the incident of Jesus being given liquid on the cross. This is all the more compelling because Luke tells us that he checked his sources carefully; and he must have known about the event, having read of it in Matthew's and Mark's accounts. If this had been the cause of death, Luke is the one who we would, in all likelihood, be expected to mention it — and perhaps even highlight it. The omission is notable for a doctor of medicine.

Asphyxia (Suffocation)

Let us say with confidence that the cause of death in all crucified victims is asphyxia. The cross was not so much an instrument of death as a tool for torturing a person to death. Its genius is to make the victim die in the greatest possible agony and to prolong that agony. The details will bear this statement out.

23

> ✝
> *The cross was not so much an instrument of death as a tool for torturing a person to death.*

As the person hung on the cross, the body sank, being unable to be held up for long by the outstretched arms. (Even a healthy person cannot hold his body up for long with arms horizontal.) Once he had sunk, it created the position of upraised arms, which inhibits the normal functioning of breathing. Inhaling is easy in this position, but exhaling is difficult and becomes more and more difficult the longer the victim hangs on the cross. The strongest muscles are for inhaling and the weaker ones for exhaling, because exhaling is normally a function of the stretched lungs contracting and the chest cavity doing likewise. It's almost automatic and effortless. In this position, hanging with upraised hands, we need to have strong muscles to exhale; but they are not strong enough to perform well and fight the weight of the body.

The result is that the normal oxygenation of the blood, which takes place in the lungs when we breathe, is greatly diminished due to the stale air being trapped in the lungs.

Less oxygen for the blood means less for the muscles. Less oxygen in the muscles means a build up of carbonic acid in the muscles, and this triggers a rush of painful conditions.

First, the heart has to work harder and, as a result, it beats faster. Being a muscle, it becomes weaker with each strained beat. Death is threatening. Muscle fibers are also provoked by the lack of oxygen and become excited. They cramp (I'm using lay terms), and we all know the pain of cramp, particularly if you can't stretch the limb in the opposite direction and can't do anything to relieve it. The crucified victim had no relief. **All the large muscle masses would start cramping and the body would distort in untold agony.** The contractions, after a few hours, became violent. The only way to ease the condition was to pull up on the nailed hands and press up against the nailed feet to expel the stale air in the lungs; and then to take a new breath, after which the victim would sink; and the cycle of insufficient oxygen would start all over again. **Terrible pain was brought on — breath after breath.** The victim, even if in good health, could not keep this up indefinitely and would eventually sink for the last time and die.

The lack of being able to breathe normally felt like a very bad attack of asthma. Another way of describing the feeling is to think of how you might feel if you were being strangled or suffocated. Let's say it again. **All the crucified died of suffocation — asphyxia.**

In the final stages, when the victim can raise himself no more, the face reddens and turns a violet color, while the body sweats enormously, staining the ground below. Then, convulsing, the body stiffens in death.

The Ultimate Proof of Love

Come with me again to that rocky outcrop outside Jerusalem on a Friday's mid afternoon in 33 AD. The crowd has turned ugly with its taunts and jeers. Religious authorities are leading and encouraging the violence and cruelty and are throwing what insults they can. A mother is weeping uncontrollably; and the Roman soldiers are going about their duty, hardened by their familiarity with the executioner's skills. The cries of pain are numbing, and even the birds have left to sit sadly at a distance, confused at what they sense. The air is still before a violent storm breaks with fury over the spot where Jesus is dying.

Suddenly, as he struggles in anguish, lifting himself up for one more breath — one more much needed life-giving breath — his voice can be heard ringing with a purity that stings the souls of the taunters and mystifies the soldiers, *"Father, forgive them for they don't know what they are doing!"*

Do you understand what you hear? Do you appreciate what you see? You have just heard and seen the extreme depths of God's own heart!

> ✝
> "Father, forgive them for they don't know what they are doing!"

God loves all who hurt him and blaspheme him. I say it again: God loves all! He loves sinners — those who make mistakes — those who hate themselves, those who try to kill him or simply ignore him. He loves the terrorist, the rapist, the murderer. He loves you, me! With the very breath he needed to assuage his own pain, Jesus prayed for our forgiveness and hurt all the more because he used a life-giving breath that would ease his pain to pray for us instead! **It cost him dearly to pray for all the people.**

"Where was God in all this carnage that was inspired by the hatred of a man so good?" we cry. God was there that day — nearer than he has ever been to his creation, unseen by all faithless eyes, but glimpsed at least by the Centurion who blurted out, *"Surely this was the Son of God."* He was there in his mother's hurt, hurting with her, without camouflage. He hurts in all *our* hurts.

Stay with me. Sit on a rock. There's one over there. Just look until your eyes see with the clarity of your heart. And while you sit and look in wonder, think with me...

Inevitable Love

This was not an act of love arising out of a "decision" to show us how much he loved us. God didn't meet with technicians in Hollywood to plan a dramatic showcase of love, complete with technical effects in order to convince the world that he loved all of its inhabitants. It was not his purpose to convince anyone. Nor was it an act of love arising out of a decision to save us. This was not a decision of the Godhead at all!

What we see when we read about the death of Jesus and feel his love is the love of God that *had to love* because he *is* love and he couldn't do anything *but* love us. It was the natural way God would act: love us with everything he is. It was God being God. It is as though Christ couldn't help himself. It was what John talks about in 1 John 4:7-10.

> ... *love comes from God. Everyone who loves has been born of God and knows God. Whoever does not love does not know God, because God is love. This is how God's love is seen among us: He sent his one and only Son into the world that we might live through him. This is love, not that we loved God, but that he loved us and sent his Son as an atoning sacrifice for our sins.*

We are gazing on the true expressive nature of God that surfaced at Calvary in a pure and irresistible form. We are looking right into the exposed heart of God.

Where is the anger because people wouldn't believe him? Where is the fury over men beating his Son and driving nails through Destot's space, creating such horrible pain? Where is the divine wrath? Don't we feel God would have been greatly provoked and simply *had* to respond in fierce justice when they started driving nails into his Son? To our amazement he does not. He is not threatening, avenging or even scolding. He even keeps his angel hosts in restraint. (How they must have longed to be let loose!) Look carefully, and all you will see is God loving — true to his nature. What kind of a God is this?

Or perhaps we are philosophizing that this God is off on some holiday or is more likely unconcerned with what we do — a God so remote and uncaring that he seems to be dead. That's unlikely, since we then must assume that he doesn't care for his Son either.

We have to conclude that this is the act of a God who simply *is* love — one who is behaving according to his irrepressible nature. This is also a God who not only *is* love but is *defining* love before our very eyes for even the spiritually blindest among us to see. It means

> ✝
> *...a God who simply is love — one who is behaving according to his irrepressible nature.*

that you and I are not, and never will be, beyond the love and care of God. No matter what we do, we can't offend his love so badly that he ceases to love us. Jesus is being true to his words: *"Love your enemies, do good to those who hate you..."*

We have a lesson here in the true nature of love.

Transforming Love

When love rises to go beyond what we expect, can imagine, and can even understand, it becomes a challenge. It calls us to a higher plateau of living. It speaks directly to our limitations, saying, "Even though you — a limited creature who can only be in one place at a time and can't leave your restricting body — <u>you</u> can let God take you beyond your body and all your limits to taste his liberating love. Will you accept the challenge?"

> ✝
> *...<u>you</u> can let God take you beyond your body and all your limits to taste his liberating love.*

28

Many have!   Like Mother Teresa, or the unnamed hordes of people who have, for a glorious moment, loved like Jesus loved and challenged all of us.   Lives are transformed when they accept the highest challenges and bury their self-centeredness, rising to live with a God-centeredness.   In all your acts of love, try to love like God, not like some earthly limitation or misrepresentation of his love.

In the name of this kind of love we fight injustice, make a heaven out of our homes, touch the untouchable, sacrifice our comforts for the Kingdom of God, and discover the eternal joy of God's way of living. And as though it were a side effect of all this fulfilling activity, we find our self-esteems lifted, which in turn helps us love even more.   Remember, he wants us to have a healthy self-love because he asks us to *"Love your neighbor as yourself,"* and surely that suggests we must love ourselves in a healthy manner.

Enlightening Love

I find so many cynics consumed with the question of where evil came from. Why does evil's origin fill the screens of their curiosity? Is it because they feel there is no satisfactory answer to this question and they have a point on which they can crucify God? We have seen people's willingness to engage in that occupation, haven't we?   If I had the choice of two problems to solve — where did evil come from or where did love come from — I think I would choose to discover where love came from. The discovery would do me more good and keep me from developing a negative compulsion about evil's birthplace. I simply prefer to be mentally engaged with the positive and the good.

When asked by philosophy students "Where did evil come from?"   I always reply with another question, simply to redress the balance, "Where did love come from?"   I am aware of most theories of where love came from. The one that amuses me most is the supposed scientific answer that it is a chemical production, manufactured in the human body by certain mental conditions — similar, if you like, to the mentally manufactured desire for an ice cream — nothing more, nothing less. When I hear that I feel empty, robbed of something I treasure as far more beautiful and meaningful. If that is <u>all</u> it is, I am certainly deceived about the values of this existence. I want it to be more. My desires taunt me. So where did that want for it to be more come from?

My questions won't end till I find an answer. I am left unsatisfied and frankly unable and unwilling to live without a meaningful answer. Surely there is something more satisfying. There is! The noble love we feel, want, and occasionally aspire to, comes from our creator God. He is a God of love and the source of all unselfish love. Love is not one of the mysteries of the universe.

✝

He is a God of love and the source of all unselfish love.

Put another way, either love finds its value and meaning in some source outside ourselves (such as God) or love is a crass, ugly, meaningless deception that only torments us — a chemical urge for ice cream. If it has no meaning; if it is simply a chemical reaction that we can rationally find no satisfaction in, we should reject the false vibes it produces.

How satisfying to know that the utterly selfless love of Jesus, about which you have just read, is not a deception, but a glimpse of the Divine. How enlightening it is to know that this beautiful love is the image in which we were created and to which we can aspire with deep reward.

Selected Bibliography

The Death and Resurrection of Jesus Christ by Karl Bornhaeuser; 1958 Printed in India at the C. L.'S. Press, Bangalore 1

The Passion and Death of Our Lord Jesus Christ by Pierre Barbet 1954; Cahill and Co. Ltd.

Also by Barbet, *Five Wounds of Our Lord Jesus Christ*

Also by Barbet, *Corporal Passion of Our Lord Jesus Christ.*

The True Likeness: Hynek, 1951

Today's Handbook of Bible Characters by E. M. Blaiklock, 1979

About the Author

RAY W. LINCOLN

Ray Lincoln has served as senior pastor to single and multi-staffed churches in New Zealand, Australia and the USA. His 40 years of experience in coaching, counseling and teaching have given him the opportunity to guide many people to self-discovery and spiritual renewal. He has studied extensively in the areas of Psychology, Theology, Philosophy and Personology and has earned a BA, BD, MDiv, PhD and LTh.

Teaching people to succeed in life and overcome their challenges with God's strength are his passion. Ray says, "While remaining true to the teachings of the Bible, my strong interest has been to use the best of science and develop a true Biblical Psychology that can help people find true fulfillment. God wants this for all of us. He knows best how we function and has left us the most helpful life-manual as the best-selling book ever!"

Conducting well over one hundred seminars in Australia, New Zealand and the USA has led him to lecture in universities, seminaries, and Bible colleges as well as businesses and churches. He has mentored pastors and other professionals. Ray has a deep faith in God, strengthened by his studies, and offers his services, experience and knowledge to you. His wife, Mary Jo, is more than a willing partner in his ministry and, in her own right, contributes much to their joint mission.

Books by Ray W. Lincoln

If you prefer to read books that get right to the heart of the matter you will find them in this list. The goal in producing these monographs is to provide immediate help in an easy-to-read and quick-to-assimilate format. The topics were chosen from help most often sought by Dr. Lincoln's clients, friends and church members where he was pastor. More books are on the way! So keep in touch!

The Art of Encouragement – Everyone needs encouragement so more encouragers are needed. Do you long to be an encourager to your loved one or friend who is hurting, grieved or depressed? Learn the basic skills in this helpful guide.

Finding God's Will for You – How can I know what God wants me to do and be? Ray Lincoln has been asked this question countless times over his forty-plus years of ministry. Here, he guides his readers through fundamental steps to determining God's will and obtaining the peace and confidence of faith.

Path to Positive Internal Power – Self-esteem is the current topic of hundreds of books available these days. This guide and workbook directs the reader to improved self-esteem for themselves and gives guidance for building self esteem in children and teens.

Personal Excellence – Eleven principles to adopt from the life of Christ that will guide you to success in all your endeavors.

Willed in Heaven and Made to Work on Earth – What is the secret to a long and happy marriage? Herein is revealed the "real secret" that really is no secret at all. Using the example of the marriage of Mary and Joseph, which had all the elements to create failure, the author shows how God designed the marriage relationship to work.

"I love you," signed Jesus – The inspiring account of Christ's suffering as you have not heard it told before. First printed in New Zealand and "sold out," this scholarly study into the details of Christ's passion will stir you to love and serve the One who died that we might live.